PARENTING WITH A TOXIC PARTNER

Helping Our Kids Survive and Thrive Amidst Emotional Abuse

When our kids suffer, parenting hurts.
When our co-parent is toxic,
parenting crushes our soul.

by Renee Swanson

Parenting with a Toxic Partner:
Helping Our Kids Survive and Thrive
Amidst Emotional Abuse

Copywright 2019, by Renee Swanson

This eBook contains helpful information for a parent who is struggling with the effects that toxic parenting is having on their own kids. It is written for those parents who are watching emotional abuse have an effect on their kids. It is not meant for the purpose of diagnosing the co-parent or replacing the incredible value of professional therapy for all involved. It is not an exhaustive list of the unbelievable amount of damage these kids are suffering.

The author of this book is not a licensed therapist or counselor. She is simply sharing from her own experiences as a mother parenting with a toxic covert narcissist. She shares specific examples and suggestions for helping kids process their hurt and confused feelings. Whether you are separated, divorced, or still trying to fight your way through a marriage, this eBook will help you to become the anchor that your kids need.

You may contact the author, Renee Swanson, at
https://www.facebook.com/renee.covertnarcissism
renee@universallyus.com
www.universallyus.com
www.covertnarcissism.com

CONTENTS

ASSESSING THE SITUATION
Making Sense out of the Chaos

INTRODUCTION

Parenting is not easy. I have often said that it is not for the faint of heart. It is the single hardest thing I have ever done in my life. At the same time, though, it is the single thing that has taught me more about life and about myself than anything else.

I would not trade being a parent for anything in the world! While it is the most challenging thing, it is also the most rewarding.

If you are here, reading this, then you are wondering if something is wrong in your specific situation. Our world is full of abusive parenting. It is FAR too common and extremely painful.

Narcissism plays a huge role in toxic parenting. Learning about narcissism and the many different aspects of it is incredibly helpful on this journey.

Some types of abuse are easy to see while other types are much more hidden. Physical abuse and sexual abuse is easier to see and easier to identify, but not all abuse is visible on the outside. Much of the abuse is covered and hidden. This comes out as emotional abuse, verbal abuse, mental abuse, and psychological abuse. In addition, physical abuse is often accompanied by more hidden abuse too. But the hidden abuse is not always accompanied by outward

1

physical abuse, leading to much confusion and self-doubt.

Just because the bruises aren't visible on the outside does not mean the bruises aren't there. The internal bruises are extremely painful and damaging. They often take much longer to heal.

When our kids suffer, parenting hurts. When our co-parent abuses our kids, parenting crushes our soul.

If your partner is abusive, then you are NOT co-parenting. You are counter parenting.

In this unit, we will explore what this looks like so you can get a better understanding of your own situation. The specifics of every family will certainly look different. But abuse is abuse and carries a whole lot of common characteristics.

Let's get started.

SIGNS OF TOXIC PARENTING

Toxic parenting is sometimes very easy to identify, while at other times it goes unnoticed for years.

Often it is easiest to spot by observing the thoughts, feelings and behaviors of the family members around that parent.

Here are some things to look for in the suspected parent, in the family, in you, and in your kids.

The signs of toxic parenting show up in everyone in the household. In fact, they are often easier to see in the victims of the abuse than in the abuser. Abuse can be extremely covered and difficult to see, leaving much confusion in the minds and hearts of those involved.

The environment created by a toxic parent is incredibly unhealthy and damaging. It is a place where there is no emotional safety for anyone in the household. This environment does not show up overnight. It is created gradually over time. The outbursts, rages, and victim cries of a toxic parent cause everyone to start tap-dancing around them. It starts with one single episode, one single day. But the cyclical nature of it causes this to become the norm without anyone ever even realizing it.

Let's look at all the individual roles involved and the signs to look for.

SIGNS IN THE TOXIC PARENT

If you suspect that your child's other parent might be toxic, then I recommend you spend some time truly observing their actions, words, and interactions. Practice watching without reacting. Try your best to consider their behaviors without your own emotions getting involved. This is not easy, but you can do it with some practice.

Experts have built many lists of the common traits seen in a toxic person. Go through this list and check the ones that apply in your situation.

- Superiority

A toxic parent portrays an air of superiority. No one else is more capable of anything than them. No one else can explain anything better, can communicate anything better, or can do anything better. They always have something to teach or show because they are the so superior.

- Entitlement

Toxic parents expect to receive what they want and when they want it. "No" is never okay with them. Even "not yet" or "wait" is beneath their status. They feel entitled to anything and everything because of their superiority.

- No reciprocity, no give in the give-and-take of normal life

You always owe them, but they never owe you. They feel entitled to respect, courtesy, and compassion. But they carry absolutely no responsibility to reciprocate that back to you.

- No reconciliation

Problems happen in every relationship. We all do and say things we shouldn't have. This is normal. But when you are with a toxic person, these occurrences become monuments in your relationship. There is simply no ability to make peace with them. Forgiveness and reconciliation never happen.

- Circular conversations

Round and round and round. You are looking for closure over a specific occurrence, but the closure never comes. These conversations can last for hours on end, often into the middle of the night. Things get brought up that have absolutely nothing to do with the topic at hand. Words get twisted, and things taken out of context. Fancy words get used that have no meaning, just to confuse you. You head is spinning wildly with no idea how you got here. You finally wave the white flag, give in and possibly even apologize to them.

- No apologies ever

Genuine apologies never come. There is always an excuse, a reason, or a manipulative plan. The words, "I'm sorry," are to get you to shut up, take them back, or prove how good of a person they are. They are often, if not always, followed by reasons that it's all your fault.

- No genuineness

Everything is manipulated, contrived, controlled, and fake. Nothing seems real. You may feel you are trying to communicate with a computer rather than a person.

- No ability to take personal responsibility

A toxic person has a very difficult time with any feelings of vulnerability and shame. They adamantly resist these feelings and thus are unable to accept any personal responsibility for something bad. Even the smallest things can create huge reactions that seem completely out of proportion.

- No compassion or empathy

The ability to empathize with another's feelings is painfully absent in a toxic person. When you try to address your own feelings with them, the conversation always swings back to them and their own hurt feelings. The emotions of another person simply do not seem to register with them.

Just because some of these signs are present, it does not mean that the parent is in fact a toxic parent. Everyone has some forms of these traits, and everyone goes through phases where these traits are more prevalent than normal. With a narcissist, however, these characteristics are constantly present and never recognized by that individual. The intense lack of empathy and genuineness prevent them from ever truly recognizing their own behavior and its effects on others. Non-narcissistic individuals self-reflect, catch themselves, and improve over time. Narcissistic people do just the opposite. They get worse over time and more convinced of their right-ness.

SIGNS IN THE FAMILY

Sometimes it is easier to determine the existence of toxicity in an individual by the thoughts and behaviors of those around them. Be sure to take some time to explore your own feelings and the feelings of your kids and other family members.

You might be living with a toxic partner if some of the following things are true within your family.

*You are spending large amounts of energy keeping that parent happy, or at least not angry. In addition, you often feel like you never succeed at this.

*You become a purpose-driven family focused on not upsetting that particular parent. This is often unspoken, just accepted.

*You are instinctively trying not to attract his/her attention, never knowing if that attention will be positive or negative.

*You experience being "trapped" or "targeted" by that parent.

*The kids consistently disappear when he/she is around.

*No one feels safe to have open conversation in the same room as him/her. Talking stops when they enter the room and pick back up when they are gone.

*That parent's thoughts, feelings, and opinions matter more than anyone else's in the family. Everyone else is willing to keep their own opinion to themselves in order to not have to deal with that parent's responses and attitudes.

*Everyone feels like nothing is ever good enough for him/her.

*Making him/her upset causes everyone to be miserable. It ruins the entire day.

*No one wants his/her help. It just isn't worth the price you have to pay.

*Something is not quite right, but it is extremely difficult to pinpoint exactly what it is

When one person in the family is causing the family to not function as a unit, this is toxic and abusive. It takes its toll on everyone involved. When normal, everyday conversations start happening in private whispers, this is a huge sign that something is really wrong.

SIGNS IN YOU

Dealing with a toxic partner for a co-parent is an absolute nightmare. While you may be focused on your kids, you are not exempt from the pain and its effects.

Here is a list of signs to look for in yourself.

- Extreme emotional exhaustion, a feeling of emptiness that goes to your very core
- Extreme mental exhaustion, your brain is tired of all the over-thinking and over-analyzing
- Feeling that everything is your responsibility to fix
- Feeling that everything is your job
- Finding yourself working overtime to build a relationship between that parent and his/her own kids, even feeling that this is your responsibility
- Constantly monitoring that parent's thoughts, feelings, and moods
- Being afraid to voice your own opinions and thoughts around him/her
- Pushing your own feelings inside rather than express them to him/her
- Feeling that you have to undo the work of your co-parent
- Feeling that you have to clean up his/her mess in relation to the kids

- Making mental arguments and counter arguments with him/her before conversations ever even happen
- Afraid to leave your kids with that parent
- Eager, almost panicked, to get back to them to see what damage has been done, often feeling guilty for taking any time for yourself

It is very easy to feel like everything is your fault in this type of relationship. I encourage you to reflect on your situation openly and honestly. As best you can, put your feelings aside and observe. Try to watch your home life as an outsider and consider if the interactions that are taking place are reasonable or not. Take notes. Write stuff down. Read it later when your emotions are calmer. Gaining an objective perspective is so necessary and yet so difficult as well.

SIGNS IN YOUR KIDS

Toxic parenting takes a huge toll on the kids. However, the signs in the kids are incredibly difficult to see sometimes. Most kids are not able to clearly express how they are feeling. They often suppress and run from negative feelings, simply as a natural reaction to the pain.

In addition, the signs of this damage are incredibly similar to normal developmental phases in a child's life. Let's face it. Teenagers are often not the easiest people in the world to talk to, especially as their parent. Mood swings, low self-esteem, anger, and insecurity are known signs of puberty and hormonal changes in even the healthiest of kids. At the same time, these are signs to look for in an abused child.

So how do you know the difference? This is a tough question and one that many people struggle with. In the following books, I take a much closer look at the specific types of damage being done to the kids and ways to counter it.

For now, here is a list of some of the signs of abuse in the kids.

*They ask specific questions, such as, "Why doesn't daddy/mommy like me? Why do I feel like he/she is never proud of me?"

*They experience much confusion, saying things like, "I feel that I'm a terrible person, but I don't know why."

*They express that they hate themselves or that they are worthless. They feel that they are never good enough.

*They say that they can never forgive themselves, even though they have not done anything wrong.

*Their own anger and disapproval is directed at themselves for no apparent reason.

*They carry an unusual amount of stored up anger, buried deep inside and have difficulty expressing or removing it.

*Their mind is over-thinking everything they say or do or might say or do. They over-analyze excessively.

*They are having extreme difficulty in finding a sense of self and feeling good about themselves.

ARE YOU CO-PARENTING OR COUNTER PARENTING?

One of the things you need to ask yourself is, "Are you co-parenting or are you counter parenting?" When you are co-parenting, whether you are still married or divorced does not matter. You still feel that you have a teammate. You and the other parent work together to find what is best for you children. You may have disagreements, but you are able to work through them. Both of you have your children's needs and best interests at heart.

Counter parenting, however, is when you have to actually work against the energy and intentions of the other parent to help your kids get on a healthy path. It is when the other parent does not have the kids' best interests at heart and instead is using them for their own gain. You find yourself needing to spend incredible amounts of energy undoing the damage done by the other parent on a regular basis.

Instead of a teammate, you literally feel like you have an enemy. Disagreements are your normal interactions, and working them out together is impossible. There is absolutely no give-and-take in this whole process with a toxic parent.

Now I'm not talking about the normal times of humanness when we disagree or accidentally hurt each other and our own kids. We all get a little short at times or a bit cross because of our own stress level. We all are guilty of unintentionally ignoring our own kids and their needs because of our own distractions. This is normal, not excusable, but normal nevertheless. A healthy parent knows this, recognizes this, and makes it right. They don't hide it and pretend it never happened. They absolutely don't blame it on their child. They don't make excuses and don't get defensive. They certainly DO NOT do these things intentionally and repeatedly as a means of control and manipulation. They apologize, validate the child's frustration over the situation, and work to make sure it doesn't happen again.

Toxic parents, on the other hand, consistently do damage to their kids. They stomp all over their feelings on a regular basis with no concern or regret. They have a complete lack of recognition of it and a complete inability to make it right with that child. Reconciliation never happens.

The toxic parent could be the mother or the father. In my situation, it is my boys' father. Therefore, my articles, blog posts, and books are written from that angle. This is in no way intended to imply any gender bias. I have seen many examples of toxic parenting existing in both genders.

CONCLUSION

Counter parenting with a toxic partner is extremely challenging and exhausting. It will test your patience and your stamina, in ways that you have never considered. You will feel like someone is repeatedly reading you your rights, "Anything you say can and will be used against you."

Counter parenting with my covert narcissistic husband is the hardest thing I have ever done in my entire life. Recognizing that I was in a bad situation, I poured absolutely everything I had into helping my boys. I often felt like it would be the end of me. My tank ran bone dry multiple times. There were many days that I felt like I was failing horribly and just wanted to give up. Yet other days, I seemed to be making great progress with them and found myself extremely energized.

How I was doing with all of this greatly depended on how they were doing. When they struggled, I hurt so badly for them. When they showed signs of narcissism or toxicity, I wanted so badly to give up. When they showed signs of promise and hope, my motivation instantly returned. When you are living in such an abusive environment, you are quite vulnerable to extreme ups and downs.

You must remember that you are strong enough to do this. If I can do it, so can you! Approach life one day at a time. Sometimes maybe even one hour at a time. Don't look far into your future. None of that exists yet, and all it does is take energy away from your now. Pour everything you have into the now. Give your kids all of you, right now.

The damage that kids often experience from toxic parenting can be extremely debilitating. It can haunt them and their relationships for the rest of their lives. But it doesn't have to. This damage can be reduced. Understand, though, that it may never go entirely away, just like scars that always remind us of an injury. These scars are internal and invisible.

If you are in a toxic relationship, then chances are you have become extremely good at not acknowledging your own feelings. We learn not to trust our feelings or at the very least that those feelings are not worth the price we pay for them. We learn to hide our feelings as a way to protect ourselves from harm. We are not alone. Our kids learn these lessons too.

They need our help, no matter what their age. They need to learn to reconnect with their own feelings. They need to learn to trust those feelings. They need you, not only as a role model on that, but also as a safe parent that allows them to explore their own feelings.

Research is showing that even one healthy and connected parent can make all the difference in the world for our kids. They need one parent who loves them, no matter what. One that sets healthy boundaries and gives unconditional love. One that offers forgiveness and compassion. One that builds a true relationship with them.

Open your own heart to your child. It is a high price, but it is absolutely worth that price. It is the best chance they have in life!

I wish you all the best. If I can ever be of service to you and your family, please don't hesitate to contact me. Raising kids is my life!

PERSONAL NOTES

_____

_____

_____

_____

_____

_____

_____

_____

_____

_____

_____

_____

_____

_____

_____

_____

_____

_____

_____

_____

_____

MAKING A PLAN
Creating a Strategy for Healing

INTRODUCTION

Have you ever flown on an airplane? Have you listened to the flight attendants when they do their safety talk? Do you remember what they say about the oxygen masks?

It goes something like this:

If we are up in the sky at 30,000 feet and encounter an air pressure problem, then these oxygen masks are going to fall out of the space above your head. Calmly put your mask on your face and pull the little strings on each side to make it tight. Breathe normally. The bag does not inflate, but oxygen is flowing.

Then they add:

If you are traveling beside a young child, please put your own mask on first and then assist the child.

As a mother, I know that my instincts would absolutely be to help my child first. Panic and adrenaline would hit if those mysterious masks ever fell from the sky in front of me, and my first reaction would be to help my kid.

So stop and think for a moment. Why is it that they tell us to help ourselves first? Because they realize that we need to put ourselves into a stronger position to be able to help. We need to be breathing properly in order to then calmly help them.

These flight attendants know that the parent sitting beside their child is the best person to be helping that child. But if the parent passes out, then both will need help from others. In fact, if the parent passes out, both could end up dead.

Life with a toxic, abusive or narcissistic parent works the same way. If you, as the non-abusive parent, don't help yourself, then you increase the chance that you and your kids will all go down.

You must help yourself first. You must put yourself in a healthier place in order to see straight to help your kids. If your emotions are a wreck, how in the world are you going to help your kids with their emotions? You can't!

Please listen to me. Make yourself a priority. If it makes you feel that you are being selfish, let go of those feelings right now. You are getting healthy for your kids. There is absolutely nothing selfish about that! Put your own mask on first, so you are fully prepared to help your kids.

WORK ON YOU FIRST

The absolute best thing you can do to help your kids is to help yourself first. You have undoubtedly suffered from this abuse too, and you cannot help your own kids if you are too broken down yourself.

You must build your own strength and confidence. Your kids need you to be strong. Your strength will give them the strength they need to battle this too.

Work on yourself! This is crucial. Your own inner strength will be an anchor for them. If you are a wreck from the emotional abuse you have endured, then you are of little help to your children. And yes, if you are partnered with a narcissist of any sort, then you are a wreck from the emotional abuse, at least in phases of your life. You have suffered and quite possibly still are. You must give yourself some time and attention.

When you fly on an airplane, the stewardess always goes through a safety demonstration before the flight leaves the ground. You learn how to put on your seatbelt, like we all haven't done this a million times. You learn how to use your seat cushion as a flotation device, even though you may be flying over the desert. And you learn what to do if the oxygen bag falls out of the overhead compartment above you.

What is it they always say? If you are traveling with a child, put your own mask on first! Then you can assist your child. They realize that if you pass out, then both of you are going to die. Your child is not going to be able to be calm enough, old enough, strong enough, tall enough, smart enough or whatever to take charge of the situation. So they are calling on you to be the responsible adult. Put yourself in a position to be secure enough to confidently help your own child.

I am making that same plea to you! Your child is not capable of fixing this. They are not aware enough, smart enough, calm enough, mature enough, etc. I don't care how smart they are, they do not have enough life experience to grasp what is going on. You have to get a hold of this first! Put yourself in a position to be secure enough to confidently help your own child. Put your own mask on first!

LEARN ABOUT NARCISSISM

No matter what type of abuse you are dealing with, narcissism plays a role. Start learning as much as you can about narcissism. Start reading. Much of what you read will answer a lot of your questions. You may find yourself unable to put it down.

No one learns as much about narcissism as one who is living with it. The learning is out of desperation and survival. Starved for some form of understanding, we become obsessed with reading about it. Why is this? Because finally we have some validation for the way we have been feeling for years. Finally someone else gets it. Finally we have a reason for all the confusion and exhaustion in our own minds.

One huge piece of advice - if you are going to look for a therapist, make sure it is someone who has lived through the nightmare of narcissism. This is the ONLY way they can actually understand. In your first meeting, ask them. Tell them you want to hear a bit of their story. A good therapist will honor this. You will be able to tell by how they talk about it if they understand. In just talking with someone, you can tell if they really get it or not. This is a must in order to find a therapist who will truly be able to help you and your family.

Resist the Urge to Label

As humans we are extremely quick to label things and people. Resist this urge!! Narcissism is extremely complex. To determine whether your partner is or isn't a full-blown narcissist takes a highly trained professional and months or even years of working together. Besides, it isn't really the point either.

Think about it. Whether he is or isn't doesn't really matter. What matters is how he is treating you. Whether they are just narcissistic tendencies or full-blown narcissism just doesn't matter. Either way, no one deserves to be treated this way. It is abusive and wrong. Would you stay just because a professional found them not to be narcissistic? Not if they are going to continue treating you this way. Labeling him/her doesn't change anything, so don't put your energy there.

Do not talk bad about this other parent to your kids. All the experts seem to agree that this does more damage to the child. Whether anyone likes it or not, that is still their parent. Simply let the truth speak for itself. Be there for the kids as they start learning how to put words to their own feelings. Once the kids are old enough, they will see it for themselves. Trust this and simply build your own relationship with them, one centered on love and understanding.

Narcissism is a Spectrum

Narcissism exists on a spectrum. Extremes do exist, but the majority of people are in the middle somewhere. In most cases it is not you either are or you aren't. Not a pass/fail test or an on/off switch. Narcissism is on a spectrum, and it fluctuates. Let's explain this on a number scale, 0-10.

0 - Extreme codependency - so focused on everyone else's needs that their own needs don't even exist.

10 - Extreme narcissism - so focused on their own needs that everyone else's needs don't even exist.

People who are on these two extremes (at 0 and at 10) are the pass/fail test. You either are or you aren't. They can't possibly get more extreme. In reality, this is a small percentage of people. Let's take a closer look at the other numbers on the spectrum.

People at 1, 2, and 3 still lean strong to codependency, but have a small recognition of their own needs. When they finally get worn out enough from helping others, they might have the ability to realize this and take some time for themselves. But it won't last long. Once rested, they will immediately jump back into the world of meeting everyone else's needs.

People at 7, 8, and 9 lean strong toward narcissism. But when their partner screams loud enough and long enough, they just might be able to step back and give some space to the partner's needs. It will be short-lived though, so don't expect more than a small

24

dose of humanness. Once they give a small piece of compassion, no matter how fake, they will feel even more justified in pulling all the attention back on themselves.

Then there is the middle range of 4, 5, and 6. This is where the healthiest individuals are. They might have a day that leans more in one direction or another, or a phase of life. But they are consistently able to return to some middle ground. While I'm not saying that they are perfect or that they never hurt someone's feelings, I am saying that they are able to quickly restore balance in themselves and in their relationships.

LEARN ABOUT MINDFULNESS

If you are in a narcissistic relationship, then there is a very good chance that your mind is running crazy. Narcissists are in the crazy-making business. Here are some of the crazy-making thoughts that might be going through your head:

- Constant replays of things he has said or done

- Constantly forming arguments against what he has said or done

- Constantly seeking better ways to explain yourself

- If only I could find the right words to help him understand how he is hurting me...

- If only I could explain myself better...

- If only I could teach him a better way to interact with the kids....

- If only I had said this or that....

Some of the best arguments known to mankind take place inside our own heads, and yet remain forever unheard by human ears. We are constantly forming "statements/arguments" that we wish we had said or that we will try to remember to say next time. We always know there will be a next time, so we are constantly preparing. These arguments may or may not ever be said out loud, but they are constantly repeated in our own heads. This is crazy-making!!!! You will wear yourself out.

You must stop this crazy-making business that is going on in your own head! To do this, you have to be purposeful and diligent about it.

I once asked my Facebook group, "If you didn't have to spend so much mental energy on your narc relationship, what would you be spending all this time thinking about in life?" I got a lot of different responses. Some were very positive answers - how to be a better parent, how to do my job better, God/spirituality, my family and friends, my hobbies, and so on. One person answered, "Great question, I never thought about that."

It is time to think about it. Time to take control of your own mind back! Become aware of your own thoughts and how you spend your mental energy.

Journaling

Due to the advice of a friend of mine, I started documenting everything that was going on in my home. Originally I did this for potential legal reasons, such as a custody battle. However, I quickly discovered the personal benefits. As I recorded an event, I had just given my mind the permission it needed to stop replaying it over and over. I no longer had to remember it for future reference or to create my defense. It was written down. Now my mind could actually let it go.

Another great benefit was for all those times when I started doubting, yet again, my own perceptions of reality. Is it really that bad? Am I just seeing things wrong? Is he actually a good person? Am I crazy? Anytime I started questioning, and we all do, I went back to my journal and started reading. I never got far on any page before all the questions and doubts were erased. I am NOT crazy! His actions, words, and attitudes are completely unacceptable. They have piled up over all the years, and it is no wonder that I feel the way I feel.

Meditation

Don't run away from this one! I'm not preaching any sort of religion or spirituality here. You can go to other sources for any of that that you choose. I'm not prescribing a certain doctrine or belief. I'm not even referring to any particular techniques, postures, or breathing cycles.

I'm simply talking about purposefully calming your mind down. Have you ever tried to calm a 2-year old child to get them ready to sleep? Or even to just get them to be still for a few minutes in the middle of the day? They are all over the place with an explosive energy level. You might pick them up, hold them close to you, and simply try to spread some calm energy from you to them. In an attempt to calm them, you might find yourself slowing your own breathing down, quietly talking to them in a genuinely calm voice, or even gently singing or humming. All your effort is put into settling the child down so they/you can rest.

Our own mind has the energy level of a 2-year old. It runs constantly all day long with a ton of energy, bouncing from one thought to another. Like the obliviousness of a child, we are sometimes barely aware of its activity. Be the parent. Use some calming techniques to settle it down so it, and thus you, can rest.

That's all meditation is, quiet time for your mind. Be purposeful about having some calm mental vacation time.

NOW YOU CAN START HELPING YOUR KIDS

Your own strength will help pull your kids through this. As you heal, they will learn to heal too. As you find peace, they can find it too.

They will need some additional help along the way. Let's take a closer look at that.

Now that you have put on your own oxygen mask, you can turn to your child. This process of helping them can be a bit overwhelming for someone who is trying to counter parent with a narcissist. Narcissists are extremely good at what they do, which is to damage others. Their influence can feel all-consuming and never-ending. I admit that I was definitely overwhelmed at times and felt like I was failing miserably in helping my kids. It seemed like too much to try to turn this all around. The damage just kept piling on top of itself, day after day after day. Some days, I felt that I was losing the battle. I threw my hands up and said, "I'm done," on multiple occasions. But I had an awesome support team of family and friends around me. They kept picking me up and pushing me forward. If I can do it, so can you!

EVERYONE HAS SCARS

Everyone has scars from childhood! Everyone! This realization helped me so much. Even healthy homes leave scars on children. Youngsters come into this world seeing their parents as perfect and believing every word that comes out of their mouth. As we all know, though, no one is perfect. At some point, that bubble of perfection is going to burst, and this is earth-shattering for a child. No one escapes childhood unscathed. It just isn't possible. While some of us come out more wounded than others, we all have some recovery work to do.

This thought allowed me to see that I wasn't alone here and neither are my boys. We are surrounded by people who have been wounded by childhood. It is more than okay to talk about it with each other. We need to start showing our scars!

ALL KIDS HAVE PERIODS OF NARCISSISM

If you haven't already, you will certainly see signs of narcissism in your own children. It definitely freaked me out whenever I saw it in my boys. I would scream to myself, "NO! They cannot follow in his footsteps. I will NOT allow this to happen!" It absolutely horrified me. I tended to react hard to it, because of my experiences with my husband. But these reactions did not help my relationship with my boys. So I started reading everything I could get my hands on about the cycle of narcissism. I had to stop this!

One thing that kept popping up again and again was the belief that both toddlers and teenagers are naturally narcissistic creatures. These are normal phases of development. In these ages, children are extremely self-centered and self-focused. What 2-year old do you know that isn't all about themselves? How about a teenager? This realization caused me to relax some; as I wondered how much was a normal phase and natural progression for my boys. I was now able to stop screaming inside myself every time I saw the signs of narcissism. It even allowed me to see some of these signs in myself, without totally flipping out. Just as I said in section called Narcissism is a Spectrum, we all have times when we act like a narcissist.

I have repeatedly read that narcissists are most often adults who were badly injured in childhood somewhere and somehow. In most cases, they endured some form of intense drama in the developmental years. The drama was too much for them, and they had no help in processing it. Because of this their emotional growth stopped at that point. If it happened in their early teenage years, then emotionally it is as though they are still a young teenager. They grow physically and mentally, but not emotionally.

So when my teenage son reminds me of his narcissistic father, this makes sense. It isn't my son acting like his father, but rather the other way around. It is a father acting like a teenager. It is a normal and healthy phase of development for my son, and a place of imprisonment for his father. As I became less panicked about my sons' behavior, I was able instead to focus on helping them get in touch with their feelings and grow past this phase of life. They both are doing extremely well, but they still have their days where they are overwhelmed by all of it. I am still learning how to give them just enough support and at the same time just enough space. It is a constantly moving middle road.

WATCH THEIR HEARTS

Watch your kids' emotions like a hawk. Their own emotions will tell you a lot about how they are doing internally. If their emotions come pouring out at full boil, do NOT react, judge or freak out. Give them emotional safety!! They need a place where they can feel safe to voice and explore their own feelings. One of the biggest reasons that narcissism develops in a person is because they cannot get in touch with or handle their own true feelings. Encourage them to talk on that level. How this looks definitely depends a lot on their age. Getting a teenager to talk can be one of the MOST difficult things to do.

One of the best ways to counter narcissistic parenting is to create an emotional safe zone for your child. In a neighborhood, kids are learning to start paying attention to the roads and cars. They need a safe place to do this learning, so our neighborhood speed limits are low. It is our job to provide that safe place for our children while they are learning this important lesson. This same is true of all children in a household. They need a safe place to learn to pay attention to their own feelings and the feelings of others. As we all know, these feelings are big and can be extremely overwhelming. We need to provide that safe place for them. Even more so if they don't have it in the other parent. One healthy parent is enough to make HUGE differences in the lives of our children.

CONCLUSION

You are your kids' greatest chance. Narcissism absolutely seems to be on the rise in our world. Your own awareness and strength will help your kids tremendously.

You must put the time and effort into yourself. Think of it as wanting to give your kids the absolute best version of you that you can. Make that a version of openness, genuineness, compassion, patience and unconditional love.

As you work on you, your kids will notice. I remember when my teenage son said to me one day, "Mom, you're different." When I asked him what he meant, he said, "You're more peaceful."

Even in the midst of the wild storm I was living, peace was beginning to shine through my heart. And my kids noticed.

Our kids are caught up in this storm too. They are thrown around by the turbulence, as are we. The ups and downs of a toxic home environment take their toll on everyone.

Your kids need an anchor. They need a safe parent, one that no matter what they can always count on. They need a parent who is always there for them and who believes in them. One that builds a true relationship with them. One who is genuine and present.

One of the greatest moments of hope for me came when I read some research that said that even one healthy and connected parent can make all the difference in the world for our kids.

Nothing in life has taught me more about myself and about life as being a mom. With the lessons learned, I changed. Yes, I did some things wrong along the way. I admit that wholeheartedly.

"If I had only known then what I know now...." is a phrase that has haunted me and will continue to haunt me for all my life. I can't change the past, and neither can you. But thankfully it is never too late!

Use the massive lessons that life is throwing at you. Learn and change. Be that anchor your kids so badly need! Show them by example that you are never too old to learn and grow.

I wish you all the best. If I can ever offer any words of advice, please don't hesitate to contact me. Raising kids is my life!

PERSONAL NOTES

_____

_____

_____

_____

_____

_____

_____

_____

_____

_____

_____

_____

_____

_____

_____

_____

_____

_____

_____

_____

_____

_____

THE CHILD'S CRUSHED SENSE OF SELF

INTRODUCTION

Children of toxic and/or narcissistic parents endure damage that has long-term effects on their life. The damage often happens at a psychological level and thus is deeply engrained inside them. This makes it not only incredibly difficult to see, but also quite difficult to undo.

Children who are raised in a toxic environment often never develop a healthy sense of self. They learn early in life and on a sub-conscious level that they exist only to please that toxic parent. They become absorbed with keeping that parent happy and even with winning the parent's approval. This often consumes them at such a young age that they aren't aware of it.

A healthy sense of self remains outside of the reach of these children. They don't even know what it means and certainly do not know how to attain it. They do not develop the necessary skills for setting boundaries. Thus they can easily remain a victim of this parent's toxicity well into their adulthood years, possibly forever.

Existing Only to Please the Toxic Parent

Relationships with a toxic person revolve around that person. That is plain and simple. Everything revolves around this person. Every conversation, every decision, every plan, every event. You even get to the point that every thought in your head revolves around this toxic person. It is extremely easy to be sucked into their vacuum. Often it happens so gradually that we aren't even aware of it.

So are you in a relationship with a toxic person? Are you caught in this web of toxicity? One of the best ways to start getting some clarity is to explore your own feelings and thoughts. How do you feel around this person? Ask yourself these questions:

Do you have difficulty saying no to this person?

Do you feel like you must always give in to their requests?

Is the price simply too high for saying no and not worth it to you?

Do you feel like it is your "job" to help them be happy or stay happy?

Are you reluctant to voice your own opinion when you know it will differ from this person's?

Are you afraid of upsetting him/her?

Does the quality of your interactions with this person depend upon the mood he/she is in?

Do you work the schedule of daily life around his/her schedule? Are you constantly making adjustments to your schedule, but not willing to even ask him/her to make adjustments?

Are you exhausted from the amount of emotional and mental energy you are putting into the relationship?

Do you feel that you are wearing your brain out trying to figure out the best way to communicate with him/her?

Do you feel like you never gain motivation from the relationship?

Are you constantly making excuses for them?

If you are answering yes to most of these questions, then there is a very good chance you are in a toxic relationship. If you have kids in this relationship, then I assure you that these kids are feeling this way too. Your kids are having difficulty saying no to that parent. They feel they must always give in to that parent's request. They feel that it is their job to keep that parent happy. They are reluctant to voice their own opinion, often whether they know if it will differ or not. They are afraid of upsetting that parent. They become highly alert to that parent's mood. And they too feel exhausted from the interactions. To sum these feelings up, their entire existence begins to revolve around the narcissistic parent. They have simply become an extension of that parent, and pleasing that parent becomes their single most important role in life.

THE CHILD'S LACK OF SELF

- The child is not encouraged to develop their own sense of self.

- The child does not learn how to set healthy boundaries in relationships.

As these children fall victim to living only to please the toxic parent, their ability to build a healthy sense of self truly suffers. Toxic parents have no boundaries and yet often set the rules in the home. They view their child as only an extension of themselves and offer no respect for the healthy boundaries that should exist.

Here are some of examples of boundary violations that occur. The parent goes into the child's room any time they please, without knocking or respecting the child's privacy. Even when our oldest son was 17, my narcissistic husband would still go barging into his room without knocking. Both of my sons asked him several times to please knock first. In his passive aggressive way, my husband would act surprised and say, "Oh, okay." But yet a few days later, it was like that conversation never happened. He would barge right in again.

Toxic parents search through their kids' stuff anytime they want. Bathroom doors are not allowed to be locked. Trackers are put on their phones, with or without their knowledge. Things are not discussed with respect and compassion. They are just done in an air of entitlement and control. Often these boundary offenses are done in the name of protecting the child. The acts can seem genuine and positive, thus leaving everyone confused over their own feelings of frustration.

Communication happens whenever the toxic parent wants and in whatever way they want. No consideration is given to the child's needs or desires. With absolutely no regard for big exams at school the next morning, my husband would have lengthy circular conversations well into the night hours with our kids. These conversations often left the kids angry and in tears, completely unable to sleep.

The kids are told what to think, when to think and how to think. They are not allowed to have their own feelings and thoughts. If they try to and their own thoughts are in conflict with the narcissistic parent, the children are met with overwhelming friction. The child thus does not feel safe to voice their own thoughts and opinions. The kids doubt their own feelings and carry a sense of powerlessness. They learn to fear their independent thinking.

Lack of Awareness

The worst part is that these kids are not even aware of what is really going on here! They usually realize that something is wrong. But whatever environment kids grow up in, they believe is "normal." They think it is just like everyone else, so they don't question it. They simply accept it and play out the role. As a child gets older, they may begin to realize this isn't true. But by then, many of their childhood experiences are already ingrained in their personality.

Because your kids aren't consciously aware of it, they won't be able to tell you how they feel. A lot of adults aren't even aware of the complexity of these relationships. Kids certainly don't get it. Often when dealing with toxic people, you don't even realize you are victim for an extended period of time, if ever. Some people never wake up to it and spend their life as an extension of that person.

HELPING OUR KIDS

This one is tricky. It leaves healthy parents caught in a quandary. If you don't do anything, you are going to watch as your child is gradually sucked into and trapped in a life-draining relationship. Yet at the same time, if you try to explain what is going on to a child who is too young to comprehend, this can bite you in the backside really fast. A young child will struggle to understand, which can lead to confusion and internal conflict. At the same time, you might be accused of parental alienation, poisoning your child against the other parent.

Building Relationship Skills

Your child will need some very specific skills in order to someday stand up to their narcissistic parent and speak how they feel. These skills will help them throughout all of their life with every relationship they ever have. So no one in their right mind can argue with you building healthy relationship skills in your child.

Necessary Relationship Skills

Learn that it is okay to get angry with someone you love.

Learn to verbalize your feelings.

Speak how you feel without being unnecessarily mean or attacking.

Be honest without being rude.

Be specific and to the point. No "extra" words.

Don't demonstrate someone else's words or actions back to them.

Don't exaggerate as you talk with someone about their words and actions.

Take a Closer Look

Kids need to learn that it is okay to get angry with someone they love. When my son was 6, we were moving to another state. About a month before our move, he was playing with his best friend. He had gotten mad at his friend over some typical little kid spat. I heard him angrily yell, "I'm glad we are moving, so I can get away from you!" The other mom and I were completely shocked. This really hurt his friend.

As the two moms stepped in to help resolve this, we discovered deeper feelings. Yes they had a little spat, but it wasn't actually the core problem. Both of them were angry at being separated because we were moving away. Their hearts were in pain, but they did not know how to voice that. As we talked through this, the two boys grabbed each other in a genuine embrace. Through a lot of tears, they told each other how much they were going to miss each other. This was a great lesson that it is okay to get angry with someone you love. It doesn't mean you don't love them anymore.

Kids need to learn to speak how they feel without being mean. This is not easy to do, and kids do not do it naturally. They need to learn to be honest without being rude. The best place for them to learn these lessons is in a relationship where they feel emotionally safe. In other words, with you. Encourage them to express their feelings when they are angry with you or hurt by you. Every parent hurts their child's feelings, many times. It's okay, we all do it.

Give them the freedom to learn these valuable skills with you. When they tell you that what you did upset them, don't turn on them. Don't be defensive or easily offended. If appropriate, simply apologize for hurting their feelings. Use this as an opportunity to build more trust. Trust that you will listen to them, reflect honestly with yourself, and talk to them with compassion and empathy.

If they are expressing meanness and rudeness, help them to see that. Don't REACT back! This does NOT help teach them. This does not help them to see! Do not give them object lessons for their meanness. It will only shut their feelings down and cause more hurt and distance.

Do not take offense at everything they say. Remember, they are learning and hopefully so are you! You must work to be in control of your own emotions. Practice what you are trying to help them learn. It's okay to be angry with someone you love, but you still need to work at communicating with compassion. Speak how you feel without being mean.

What if you think they are being overly sensitive? No problem. You also get to practice being honest without being rude. Tell them what you think. Don't get angry about it. It is okay to say, "Hey I'm sorry I hurt your feelings. That is not what I meant to do. In my opinion, I do think you are perhaps being a bit too sensitive, but I am sorry nonetheless." It is okay to apologize, even when you feel you did nothing wrong.

We do it all the time. Think about it. When you accidentally bump into someone, what do you say? A toxic person is quick to blame it on the other person and snap something mean at them. But a healthy and compassionate person is quick to say, "Oh, excuse me. I'm sorry." You didn't do anything actually wrong. But that's not the point. The point is that you are able to accept the blame and apologize. The same is true when we hurt someone's feelings by mistake. Teach this to your kids.

Teach them to be specific and to the point. They need only to express how they feel and then stop, giving the other person a chance to talk. Teach them not to drag it out. You want them to learn to say, "You hurt my feelings," without going into great discussion and explanation. These discussions and explanations easily get ugly and convoluted. Extra words lead to excuses, justifications, accusations, and exaggerations. These extra words are the birthing ground for circular conversations.

Teach your kids not to demonstrate back to someone. Picture a child saying to another child, "You hit me like this," as they swing at the kid. Now how is that strike going to come out? The far majority of the time it is going to be much harder and more aggressive than whatever happened first. This is because it is loaded with more emotion. It is not possible to actually demonstrate what has happened without the feelings of being hurt involved. When we try, it never goes over very well. Teach them to say, "I didn't like it when you hit me," without demonstrating.

Demonstrating doesn't work in speaking either. When one kid says to another, "But you said, "I don't have to play" in a squeaky, obnoxious and irritating voice, this only offends the other person. The other kid quickly retorts, "I didn't say it like that." It is not possible to actually repeat something back in the manner in which it was delivered. If it has upset you, that state of being upset will cause your voice to exaggerate. So teach your kids not to imitate the voice or actions, but rather to just state how it made them feel.

Teach them not to exaggerate. It is okay to say that something upset you. You don't have to make it bigger than life in order to justify your own feelings. It is okay to be upset. "You did this 100 times," never sits well when in reality it was 5 times. Five times is enough, sometimes even one time is enough, to justify being hurt or upset. Don't exaggerate. Practice speaking the truth, as best as you can.

Don't Let the Crankiest One Make the Rules

Do not teach your kids to just keep peace because the crankiest one in the house makes the rules!! This is hard. When the crankiest one is happy, then everyone can breathe a little easier. When they are mad, life in the home can be truly miserable. We bow down to their wishes, not because we agree with them, but because we so strongly desire the peace that then comes. But it comes at too high of a price!

47

Think about what this really is teaching your kids. It teaches them to give in to the bullies, and it also teaches them to become a bully. They will learn that they need to be the crankiest one in the house, so everyone will bow down to their wishes. Kids aren't dumb. They will do this without even being aware of it. They will likely start acting like the toxic parent just so they can get their own way too. Before you know it, you will be working double-time to keep peace, not only with your narcissistic spouse, but with your own child as well.

When to Fight and When to Step Aside

As the counter parent, do not try to convince your child to just put up with it or that it's OK. Do not encourage them to stuff it under the rug. That's what we are all experts at, and it is not a healthy approach. This is simply not OK. Setting healthy boundaries with others is not only good for your relationships, it is also vitally necessary.

Your child's ability to understand and set boundaries depends largely on their age and maturity. Your younger kids will not be able to do this yet and will need you to go to bat for them. When their narcissistic parent has crossed what you think are reasonable boundaries, then you will need to step in. This is not easy, and it is exhausting. But you must dig in and do it. Choose your battles wisely though. You can't possibly fight every battle that will come your way. Some things are more important than others. You have to decide in your own given situation.

One extremely necessary thing to realize is that as your kids get older, you should not keep fighting their fight for them. Gradually let them start doing this for themselves. Listen to your heart and their hearts too. You will learn when it's time to step aside more and more. It is important that they learn to start setting boundaries while still living in the safety of your parenting. For me this is part of the reason why I did not divorce their father earlier. I felt like it was vitally important that I was around to offer them emotional safety while they learned how to handle him. You see, he will always be their father. So they are going to have to find a way to handle him later in life. I want to give them a solid head-start on that relationship, as I realize it will be a tricky one.

Specific Examples

Trapped in Conversations

Narcissistic parents like to feel in charge. They want to talk about what they want to talk about, when they want to talk about it. If there is a topic that the kids don't really want to talk about at the time, then this can prove to be extremely offensive to the narcissistic parent. Remember they want things on their terms, not anyone else's. The parent takes it personally and gets rather defensive. So the children feel obligated to talk with him/her. For my boys, I have worked hard to make sure they know that it is OK to say, "I don't want to talk about this right now." Or even, "I don't want to have this conversation."

If you don't know already, you must learn about circular conversations. These conversations are the most painful thing I have ever experienced in my life. They are devastating and will suck all the energy out of you. After one of these conversations with his father, I found our 14 year old son curled up in his closet floor with a stuffed animal saying, "I hate myself" over and over. If their narcissistic parent traps your children in a circular conversation, then they must know what this is and what to do about it. First and foremost, you must learn yourself. Read about circular conversations. Identify them and learn what to do about them. You have to take charge of these conversations. A narcissist will never end this conversation. They will go round and round and round for hours on end, attacking you both overtly and covertly. You will start by asking him about something he did and find yourself defending everything you have ever said or done. It is unbelievable! You have to be the one to stop it. You simply say, "I'm done," and walk away. Do NOT try to find closure or reconciliation. This may sound harsh, but trying to find reconciliation only keeps you trapped in this conversation for longer. This is exactly what the narcissist wants. Help your kids learn what these conversations are. Talk to them about it. Let them read the articles. This is not normal and healthy conversation, and they must realize that. They also must know how to get it stopped. Teach them to say, "I'm done talking now," and walk away. It really is that simple.

Invasion of Personal Space

Another example of an overstepped boundary is when the narcissistic parent feels entitled to enter the child's room anytime they please. This is with or without permission from the child and whether the child is present or not. Our 17 year old son tells me that his dad still barges into his room, even when the door is closed; opening his door anytime he pleases without ever knocking. He has pointed out to me how many times he was fussed at so hard for entering the parent's room without knocking, even if the door was already open. He got fussed at for even putting his hand on the door knob before waiting for an answer from within. Yet that same father feels entitled to enter his son's room whenever he pleases and has no need to respect his son's privacy. Kids need to feel that it is okay to want their own space and their own privacy. They need to learn that it is okay to protect that.

So what do you do? When the kids are young, this isn't too much of an issue, unless other things are going on that shouldn't be. For us, this became more of an issue as the kids started to become young teenagers. It was when modesty started to hit. It is better for the young teenagers to be the ones to speak up to the narcissistic parent, than for it to be you. They can say, "It makes me very uncomfortable when you do not knock before you come in." Or simply, "Can you please knock before you come in?" They do not need to offer a long explanation. Long explanations are simply breeding grounds for circular conversations. Keep it short, simple and honest.

Setting Healthy Boundaries with You

One of the best ways for your child to learn healthy boundary setting is for them to set these boundaries with you. I know this may not feel good to you, especially when their other parent is doing so much damage. But if they don't learn how to set positive boundaries with you, who will they learn it with? You are their best bet for them to be able to build this important skill.

It is okay for them to set these boundaries with me too! They can tell you that they don't want to talk about a certain topic. It is important as you try to show emotional growth and health by not getting offended and defensive. I had to learn this over the years. It took some time. But I eventually realized that it is not only okay, but it is also extremely helpful to our relationship too. Healthy boundary setting does not threaten the security of our relationship. Instead it strengthens it. As they begin to trust that you will honor their boundaries, they begin to trust you more. Knowing their boundaries will not be overstepped allows them to relax and lower their guard. This allows their real self to start to show through. Thus these boundaries are exactly what are needed to provide a breeding ground for a secure sense of self.

CONCLUSION

Boundaries are healthy. Building healthy boundaries is a skill that your kids need in life. While it is extremely difficult with a toxic parent around, it is also a great time for your kids to work on this skill. Give them the emotional safety they need while they work on this.

Kids need a safe environment where they can learn the many things they need to learn in life. A toxic parent is just not equipped to offer them this safety. But you are!

Be that safe parent for them. Honor their boundaries. Allow them to make mistakes. Forgive them when they overstep your boundaries. Help them build their own skills of boundary setting and boundary honoring. Love them every step of the way.

As they learn to set healthy boundaries, your child's own sense of self will grow. As their boundaries are respected, they will feel more confident and trusting. This allows them to relax more, dropping the defensiveness many kids hide behind. Then they can enjoy discovering themselves!

PERSONAL NOTES

_____

_____

_____

_____

_____

_____

_____

_____

_____

_____

_____

_____

_____

_____

_____

_____

_____

_____

_____

_____

_____

_____

THE CHILD'S DISTORTED VIEW OF REALITY

INTRODUCTION

Toxic individuals have such a distorted view of reality. Their world revolves only around their own needs, feelings, thoughts, and perceptions. They are notorious for pushing this distorted sense of reality onto everyone around them, especially their own children.

Their children become an extension of them. Their children's life is simply an addition to the toxic parent's story. They don't have a story of their own. Unless they get some help for someone, they are never given the chance to have their own story.

The toxic parent shuts down their feelings on a daily basis. The child feels completely unheard and invalidated. They hold massive amounts of confusion inside them. They can't line up the belief that their parent loves them with the feelings that the parent creates in them. So reality gets incredibly blurry.

Let's look at the picture this creates.

THE OVERALL PICTURE

Let's draw a picture of what the family looks like when a toxic parent is involved.

First, let's look at the toxic parent. Here you have a parent who only cares about their own feelings. They will say that they care about others, but their actions and attitudes simply don't match this. They are like a vacuum that is sucking the life out of everyone in the family. Most often, these are individuals who are extremely wounded from their own childhood. They have buried those wounds for so long and refused to face them, which leads to a continued cycle of abuse.

Next, you have the non-toxic parent. This parent is often consumed with trying to keep peace in this toxic situation. They are struggling to know what normal and healthy looks like. They have been targeted by someone who they believed loved them, and they are overwhelmed with their own hurt and pain. As such, they are often barely able to acknowledge the kids' feelings. Being beaten down again and again, they are certainly not the pillars of strength that these children so desperately need. They bury their wounds in order to be strong for their kids, but this is not sustainable. These buried wounds can also cause them to lash out with abusive behavior toward the kids, but they are not the ones that brought this to the home environment. They are victims, and they are wounded.

Finally, you have the kids in this environment. These kids feel non-existent and unheard. They have a toxic parent who demonstrates repeatedly that they do not care about the child's feelings. And they have a wounded parent who is too beaten down to truly help. So they start the process of burying their own feelings. The pain they carry is too big and overwhelming for them to handle without help. They believe that this is normal and what everyone feels. They learn that they are helpless and worthless. This is the birthing ground for this continued cycle of abuse, and it must be stopped.

THE UNHEARD CHILD

When dealing with a toxic parent, the child's feelings are way down on the totem pole. Their feelings are repeatedly not acknowledged. The toxic parent is entitled to say whatever they want and however they want, simply because they are the parent. No consideration at all is given to the child's feelings or yours either. They carry no remorse when those feelings are stomped into the ground.

For those of you fighting this, you truly need to hear this part! My boys' feelings were not being heard by their narcissistic father, but they weren't being heard by me either. I totally did not realize this until many years later. I was SO wrapped up in trying to keep peace that I pushed their feelings under the rug right along with everything else. I was so horrified by the anger I saw in their father that I simply could not handle any anger in them. I quickly pushed hard to remove anger from them. I sincerely thought I was doing what was best for them. I was trying to teach them to be peaceful. While that is a good thing to teach, I went about it all wrong in their

57

early years. I ended up teaching them that their own feelings don't matter as much as their father's simply because he was mean. The conclusion the kids then came to was that their feelings don't matter and needed to be buried deep inside. This definitely is NOT healthy and created problems down the road.

Another thing that kids in this situation learn is that in order for their feelings to matter to the world they need to be mean too. This is clearly not what we want to be teaching our children. When your child seems to turn into an alien full of meanness one day, you need to consider that their feelings are not being heard.

When counter parenting with a toxic parent, you must work extra hard on recognizing and validating your child's feelings. Their feelings are beaten down by one parent, and they sure don't need this to be done by two parents.

Stop Talking, Start Listening

Listen to your kids. Truly listen. Let them feel heard. Let them BE heard. Don't tell them their feelings are wrong or imply that they should feel differently about something. Don't always be quick to respond with advice or examples to every feeling they have. This only communicates that their feelings are in some way wrong and must be changed. Sometimes it is best to not respond, but just simply listen and be with them.

Too many times, my response was full of reasons why their feelings were wrong. I would try to talk them out of being angry with excuses and justifications. I tried to explain the hurt away so they would return to being happy. I know I just wanted them to be happy, and there is nothing wrong with that desire. However a shallow happiness is empty and creates long-term problems.

Keep your eye on the long run, not the short term. I was trying to change their feelings now, for the immediate present time. However, validating their anger and hurt has a much greater long term advantage. Acknowledge their negative feelings. Listen, don't fix. Tell them that you understand, that you can see why they would feel that way, and that you don't blame them for how they feel. The more you do this, the more they will trust you and trust their own feelings. This emotional safety is crucial. It will give them room to explore their own feelings and begin to grow emotionally.

Personal example

My boys were happily playing in the yard one day. Rather than just let them play, my husband was acting like a guard dog, waiting to pounce. Sure enough, our oldest made the tiniest of mistakes and this set his dad off. He exploded at our son and spent the next 45 minutes telling him how bad of a big brother he was. Our son was a wonderful brother, but he heard all the time how bad he was. After this berating, our son ran upstairs and closed himself in his room, completely shut down to the world. After a while, I went to his room. It took some effort to convince him to talk with me. But when he did, the conversation went like this:

Son: Why doesn't daddy like me?
Me: Oh, he does like you, son.
Son: No he doesn't. I never feel like he does.
Me: But I know that he does. He just doesn't express it very well. He had a rough childhood. His dad treated him very badly when he was young.

I would sometimes tell him some of the things that happened in his dad's childhood, hoping this would help him to understand. But it never seemed to help. My son's feelings, due to how his dad treated him, severely contradicted what I was telling him. These contradictions did not help.

Me: You are a wonderful brother.
Son: No I'm not. I'm a horrible brother. Dad says so.
Me: No, son, you really aren't. Your dad didn't have a brother. He just doesn't understand that relationship.

No matter how much I talked, none of this seemed to help. All he could hear were his dad's words playing over and over in his head.

Who is The Main Character?

My son did not need to hear about his dad's background at this point. In Book 3 of this series, The

Child's Crushed Sense of Self, I point out how kids of a toxic parent become an extension of that parent. This is one of the ways that this happens. The child's life is centered around the abusiveness that their parent experienced in their childhood. They are simply an extended part of the story.

Please hear this!! Your child's life is not about that parent. For my son, his life isn't about his dad. It's about him. It's his childhood, not his father's. He doesn't need to hear about how his dad feels. He needs validation about how HE is feeling. He is not a secondary character to his dad's story. He must be the main character in his own story!

I remember telling my son these words:
"You aren't a certain percentage of your dad and a certain percentage of me. You are 100% you. And you create a little more of you every single day of your life. Take this life and make it yours!"

I want to ask you something. If your relationship with your child were a story book that you were reading, who would be the main character? Is it their toxic parent? Is it you? Or is it really your child? Your child needs to be the main character of their own story book. I'm not saying they need to be pampered and spoiled. They don't need to get everything they want and do everything they want. That would only encourage any narcissistic tendencies they may have.

I am saying that when they open up to you about their feelings, let them be the main character for a while. Don't make the story about you or the other parent. It's about them right now.

After their feelings have been heard and addressed, then they might start asking why this is happening. When they are ready to ask, then they might feel more open to listening. You can then start helping them to understand their father's background. But if you try too soon, it just pushes their feelings under the rug and makes it all about their dad, once again.

Validate Their Feelings

Learning to validate your children's feelings requires time and effort. As you work on this, you will get it right sometimes and fail other times. In addition, what works one day may completely fail the very next day.

Also, don't expect to be able to validate their feelings if you haven't yet learned how to validate your own. In order to be real with them, you have to work on you first. While you are working on your own feelings, you can also begin reaching out to your kids' hearts. But please make sure that you are not neglecting your own. Be sure to read Book 2 in this series, Creating a Strategy.

One thing that truly surprised me was that, as I started validating my own feelings, validating theirs came easier and more naturally. As I got more in touch with my own heart, I began trusting my feelings more. In so doing, I also become much more accepting of their feelings. This was a major turning point for me and my boys.

Work on listening to your own heart! Look at your feelings. Invite them to come out of hiding. Observe them. Explore them. Don't judge them. Don't tell them they are wrong or bad. Learn from them. Work through them.

Find you a small support group. You must have at least a few people around you that get it. This is not always easy to find in these situations. Reach out to a trusted friend or family member. You can find a good therapist or counselor. Also, online support groups have started offering quite a bit of help to people who sometimes don't have any other means for support.

As you get more in touch with your own feelings, an amazing thing happens. You become more open to your kids' feelings. Start listening to your kids' hearts. Be open with them. Give them permission to explore their own feelings. Talk with them. Be attentive. Don't judge or "fix" them. Let them be their own main character. Along the way, share with them what you are working on in you. Let them know that you are not done growing.

You may need to change the way you are talking to them about their feelings. When things blow up with their toxic parent, as we all know it does, stop making excuses for the toxic behavior. Start validating your child's behavior. Here are some examples of things you might say:

"I'm sure it makes you feel like daddy doesn't like you when he talks to you that way. I can see why it would."

"I know it hurts when he talks to you like that."

"I imagine that didn't feel too good."

You might even simply ask: "How did it make you feel when he said....?"

Never Too Late to Change Your Approach

It took me far too long to learn some of this. At times, it is easy for me to regret that or blame myself for some of the damage. While these are very understandable feelings, they are also extremely wrong. **I DID NOT CHOOSE TO BRING THIS ABUSE INTO THE LIVES OF MY CHILDREN!** You also need to remember this. You are living in an impossible situation, and you did not pick this. Don't forget – you are a victim as well! The abuse is often not visible all at once or early on in the relationship. It comes gradually and covertly. Over time, you are tolerating and even excusing things you would never have put up with before.

But it's never too late. As soon as my eyes opened, I began to change my approach immediately. I realized right away that I was not helping my boys. This had to change! My son's feelings needed to be heard and validated, not explained away. He doesn't want to talk about his dad right then. He needs to talk about himself. He already has one parent who doesn't listen to or validate his feelings, he surely doesn't need two.

This change in me was noticed and acknowledged by both of our boys. They told me that I seemed more relaxed and more open. Our oldest told me that I changed and became more peaceful. I am eternally grateful that I changed my approach. The boys responded positively to that change. This change gave us more hope for our future than we had had in years. Remember, it is NEVER too late to help your kids!

The Struggle to Grasp Reality

Children of toxic parents hold a lot of confusion inside themselves. They have an extremely difficult time merging the love the toxic parent has for them with the way that parent makes them feel.

I have seen this play out in my own husband from his own childhood. He suffered badly as a child due to his own narcissistic father and much toxic abuse. On several occasions, he has said to me, "How can I hate my dad? He loves me." And yet turn right around and say, "My dad is a monster! How can I love him after all the horrible things he did to me and my mom?" He told me that to the outside world, they put on the appearance of being a perfect family. They "had to."

But on the inside, the family was a disaster. He told me that he never knew what reality actually was. Were they a perfect family or were they a disaster?

As he talked to me about the abuse, it is so clear to me that they were a disaster. Yet my 46-year old husband still cannot come to grips with reality. He continually runs back to his dad, still seeking his approval. He simply could not accept that his family was a disaster. He just couldn't do it, and that inability destroyed our marriage and damaged our own children.

My Child's Struggle

My 17-year old son has struggled with grasping reality. He holds two extremely contradictory things in his mind and seems to battle between them. He believes that his dad loves him. He believes that his dad has done the best that he knew how to do in raising him. At the same time, he is angry at how his dad has treated him all these years. He struggles with how his dad makes him feel day after day. These two pictures in his mind simply do not match.

So what is reality? Does his dad love him or not?

As I already mentioned, when our son was much younger, he used to ask me, "Why doesn't Daddy like me?" Many times he asked me this question. Each time, my heart broke for a son so badly wanting his dad's approval. As his awareness grew, he started answering his own question. "Why doesn't Daddy like me? Mom, he doesn't like anyone." Eventually, he realized that Daddy doesn't even like himself.

For a long time, I defended their dad to the boys. I would make excuses:
He's tired tonight.
He is stressed from work.
He doesn't feel too good tonight.
He's got a lot on his mind.

But the excuses wore off. When there is always a reason why a person is being mean, you just might have to stop and consider that maybe they are actually mean. If there is always a reason why they are being a jerk, maybe they are just a jerk. At some point, the excuses fall aside and you see the real person underneath.

Examples of Toxic Parenting

Here are a couple of personal examples on how toxic parenting affected my boys' sense of reality.

My narcissistic husband was lecturing the boys regarding their behavior about something. They were young, maybe 5 and 7. He said to them, "Now I know you are sitting there thinking I am an idiot...." And then started defending his actions to his youngsters.

Our young boys looked puzzled and unsure. I don't believe for a minute that they were sitting there thinking their dad was an idiot. But they probably were now. He just put those words right into their little heads.

He pushed his messed-up version of what he thought was reality onto his very young children. They were not old enough to grasp a version of reality for themselves.

Here is another personal example, regarding our youngest son.

Father to his son: So what are you studying in history right now?

Son to father: Oh, everything! (In an exhausted voice from all the homework)

Before our son could continue, his father jumped his back and yelled, "You never answer me with real answers! Can't you ever just answer my questions?"

Our son told me later that he thought he was answering his question. He was feeling overwhelmed at the amount of work he was doing, and so it felt like they were studying everything. When his dad flared up, he shut down and avoided the conversation completely. So here lies the confusion in his mind: "Do I not answer him with real answers? Are my feelings not real answers? What is a REAL answer?"

Don't Bad Mouth the Toxic Parent

One word of advice is that no matter how easy it would be, don't bad mouth the toxic parent to your kids. This only adds to their confusion and certainly does not help the situation. I'm not saying to make excuses for that parent either. This also doesn't work.

Simply let the truth speak for itself. Your children are not blind. They will see it for themselves. You can ask how they feel. You can listen to their thoughts. Let them talk and express what they see. When my son asked why his dad doesn't like him, it might have been better for me to answer something like, "Tell me what happened. How did that make you feel?" After hearing them, you can validate them by saying, "I can see why you don't like feeling that way." None of this is a direct attack at the other parent and yet confirms your child's feelings.

To continue teaching them compassion, you can follow this with, "Do you think you have ever made someone feel that way?" But don't do this until you are sure that they have felt heard and validated. Wait until they are ready to move on in the conversation.

By all means, get them talking about their feelings. Their feelings are their current reality more than anything else in their world. But you don't have to add any fuel to their anger at the other parent.

What is Reality?

Reality is not some truth out there that we all are searching for. Reality is based on perspective. Changing one's perspective changes everything. I have said this many times in life. If you change your perception of something, then everything about it changes. So what is reality? It is your perspective. How you feel about something is your reality. You may love spiders, and this is your reality. Your friend may be terrified of spider, and this is their reality. Reality is subjective.

I am sure that the reality of the Cold War is different for Russian students studying it than it is for American students. Reality is based on your own perceptions of life, and these are based on your current knowledge, awareness, feelings and other extremely subjective things.

Don't try to tell your kids what reality is. Your reality is only your own perspective and might be completely contrary to theirs. Part of why toxic parents confuse their kids so much is because they push their own perception of reality onto their kids.

Your reality might be that you are dealing with a toxic spouse. You have the knowledge and awareness to understand this reality. But your kids don't and thus this is not their reality. It certainly isn't the reality of your spouse. Your kids' reality is that they are trying to grow up and learn what life is all about. Their reality might also include that they are struggling to get along with their parents, one or both, but they don't have the life-experience to grasp narcissism (at least not in its entirety).

Work on learning their reality. It lies inside them, not outside. Dig in to their feelings and perceptions. As I mentioned before, don't judge those feelings and perceptions. Don't tell them that they are wrong. Feelings aren't wrong. They are just feelings. They also aren't permanent. Help your kids to start seeing their own reality. Help them to voice how they feel. Encourage them to voice their own perceptions.

Reality changes constantly and so do feelings. As the young teenager knows, one day "she" loves me and one day "she" loves me not. Teach them that reality is fluid and constantly changing, sort of like a river. They will function much better in life if they are flexible and fluid like that river.

The Perspective of a River

A river constantly twists and turns. Sometimes it is deep and other times shallow. Sometimes calm and other times extremely rough. You cannot describe it only one way because somewhere else it is certainly the opposite.

For your own safety and pleasure, float down the middle of that river. Ride whatever comes your way. If you get too close to the edges, you might find problems. You might beat yourself against the rocks in a fast flowing part. Or you might stall out and get stuck in the stagnant water of a calmer part. Don't float on the edges. Find your way in the middle of the river. But don't think that once you find the middle your work is done. The river turns, and the middle moves. You have to stay engaged with the river. You have to stay aware and actively directing your boat.

Such is life. Don't coast. Be purposeful about your course. Don't drift to the edges. Life will shift around. Stay engaged with it and accept it. Shift with it and keep moving forward.

CONCLUSION

If you are parenting with a toxic parent, then you are a victim right along with your kids. Breaking out of this abusive situation takes awareness and great effort.

Work on you first so you are then in a position to help your kids. Validate your feelings. Listen to them. Work on feeling heard by a small support group. As you begin to heal, you will instantly become more open to the needs of your children. You will feel more connected with their feelings because of the new connection with your own.

Remember, your kids already have one parent who is shutting down their feelings. They do not need two parents doing this!

Perspective is everything in life. Their perspective is their reality. Don't deny them this. You can help them to see that perspectives change, and as such reality changes.

PERSONAL NOTES

_____

_____

_____

_____

_____

_____

_____

_____

_____

_____

_____

_____

_____

_____

_____

_____

_____

_____

_____

_____

_____

_____

_____

THE CHILD'S CRIPPLING INTERNAL THOUGHTS

INTRODUCTION

When living with a toxic parent, the child's feelings are often telling them that something is wrong. Kids want to believe the best about their parents. They don't want to believe that their parent is bad or hates them. In fact, kids don't even consider this possibility. When they feel bad in the relationships, the child subconsciously concludes that everything must be their fault and/or that their own feelings must be wrong. So they believe that they themselves are either worthless or malfunctioning.

For obvious reasons, kids don't like how this feels, so they simply turn those feelings off. They bury them deep inside. They often are too ashamed to talk with anyone about them. These feelings can lay dormant in them for years, sabotaging their relationships without their awareness of it.

All of this is especially confusing if one or both parents are telling them life is wonderful, when it is so clearly not. In order to help your kids get honest with their feelings, you must get painfully honest with your own first.

CRIPPLING INTERNAL THOUGHTS AND FEELINGS

Kids of toxic parents carry some devastating internal thoughts and feelings. These can haunt them for many years. They can greatly interfere with their personal relationships and overall happiness in life. Here are some of those thoughts and feelings.

- Debilitating self-doubt
- Feeling "not good enough"
- Unable to give credit to self when deserved
- Belief that he/she is unworthy and unlovable
- Unbearable amounts of shame and humiliation
- Feeling worthless and hopeless

I want you to take a minute and look at yourself. You have been in a relationship with a toxic person. How has this relationship affected you? Are you stronger, more confident, feeling more loved and lovable than when you started this relationship? I venture to say that the answer is absolutely NO! Toxic people are extremely good at making those closest to them feel unworthy and unlovable. They leave you feeling not good enough, not only for them, but for anyone else either.

Now consider your kids. This abuse has not been limited only to you. If they have ANY interactions with the toxic parent, then they have picked this up too. Problem is kids think it's normal and accurate. Young kids have no basis of comparison. They think that their world is the normal for everyone. How they are treated by their parents is what they think exists everywhere. Well, if their parent makes them feel unloved, then everyone will make them feel unloved. If their parent thinks that they are unworthy, then everyone must think that they are unworthy. And so on.

Kids do not know that this is wrong and abusive. Their parents are their care-givers and their dominant source of love and happiness. When that relationship gets screwed up, it does incredible amounts of damage.

Truth be told, this is incredibly hard to combat! You can pour everything you have into it and still feel like you are failing disastrously. I know I went through this! Part of the problem is that kids, and teenagers in particular, naturally go through phases of self-doubt and feeling not good enough, even in the healthiest of homes. Add to this a toxic home and the complications multiply.

AWARENESS IS KEY

For everyone involved, awareness is key! Awareness for your toxic partner is tough. If you are in the phase of your relationship where you are still convinced that you can help the toxic parent change, I can honestly say that I completely understand. I've been there too. It took years of intense effort, a ton of energy and buckets of tears before I was finally willing to say that he will never see it. So do what you need to do. If your partner starts to accept what you are saying and makes some changes, great! You will be energized by this. But if they cannot change or continue returning to the abusive behavior, then you will run dry. When you hit rock bottom, you will know it. Then you will be ready to pour all your effort into yourself and your kids and stop pouring it into your toxic partner.

You can't force awareness in your kids. You can't "make" them see it, and you don't have to. They already do. But you do need to help them make sense of it. Kids know that something is wrong at very young ages. They don't understand what necessarily, but they don't like the feelings they have in their system. They respond to what feels good to them and what doesn't. They just don't understand it yet.

At a very young age, they learn that some topics are not safe to discuss or that some things are not safe to say. A few sharp snaps from a parent teach them a ton. "I'll never bring that up again," runs through their heads. It is amazing how young kids learn to not be honest about their thoughts and feelings. We think they learned this from society, but they learned it from us. We are very good at teaching our children how to "sweep the dirt under the rug." Many of us teach by example.

BE A SAFE PARENT

Kids need a safe place to talk about and express their feelings. They need a place where they will not be judged or analyzed. They need listeners who will not be offended and quickly defensive. They need a safe parent with whom they are free to talk out loud about anything. Learn to be that safe parent.

So what are some of the reasons we are unable to provide that safe place for our kids? Here are some, but I am sure you can add more of your own.

- You are still sweeping the dirt under the rug, still trying to keep peace with the toxic parent, still hoping that they will change.

- With the best of intentions, you might be trying to help them build a relationship with the toxic parent. We want our children to be "good" children, so we are still trying to teach them to respect their parents. We don't want to let them talk bad about their father/mother. Therefore we try to convince them of good qualities and shove the bad qualities back under that same old rug.

- Maybe your kid's feelings scare you. Anger in our own child is not a pleasant experience. So we shove their dirt under the rug too. We sure do have a lot of dirt under all these rugs.

- Perhaps you are just overwhelmed and simply don't know what to do.

HOW DO YOU HELP THEM?

You love them! You hold on to a healthy relationship with them for all your worth. You don't give in, no matter what. You will hit walls of frustration that you never even knew existed. You will hit levels of exhaustion that have never been on your radar before. But you keep pushing through! You keep on loving them.

Obviously you can't always or even often change the behavior of our toxic counter parent. So you have to focus on your own parenting skills. The goal is to create a healthy sense of self in your child. As yourself, what does this look like?

- Self-awareness
- Self-perceptiveness
- Self-value
- Acceptance of personal strengths and weaknesses
- Acceptance of one's humanness

Don't Over-Compensate

I want to start with a warning. When our co-parent is abusing our children in any way, it is extremely easy to over-compensate by trying to erase all the bad feelings in our child. Our intentions are good. We know that those bad feelings are coming from the way they are being treated. So if we can erase those bad feelings, then maybe we can erase the damage they are suffering. However the results may not be quite what we hope for.

Let's take a closer look at the narcissistic personality specifically. **One definition of a narcissist is an empty shell wrapped in a façade of grandiosity**. That empty shell comes from all the abuse, but the façade of grandiosity comes from the over-compensation.

Empty Shell

Kids cannot emotionally comprehend the abuse of a parent who is supposed to love them. They internalize it, believing that they themselves are to blame. This leaves them feeling worthless and hopeless. These feelings are too overwhelming for kids and leave them numb. The kids then often close off to their own feelings in self-preservation. In other words, they become an empty shell.

Façade of Grandiosity

When the other parent over compensates by telling them how wonderful, beautiful, amazing and so on that they are, this does not line up with the empty feelings they are experiencing. But it feels better, so they try to cling to this. However, this then becomes a false sense of security for them. It is often easier to ignore bad internal feelings than it is to face them. So it is easy to cling to those feelings that they are great and wonderful, even though they don't truly believe them. They become that empty shell wrapped in a façade of grandiosity.

Don't Fix Them

One thing you must do as the safe parent is give your kids the freedom to talk to you. Don't react, simply listen. Let them express their feelings, even uncomfortable ones. They might even express frustrations about you. That's okay. In fact, that's great! Toughen yourself up so that you can handle it. They may say some hurtful, angry and painful things. That's okay. If they can't express their feelings to you, who are they going to express them to?

When kids are trying to get more in touch with their own feelings, their filters don't work as well. When they yell, "I hate you," try to remember this is coming from their feelings. Most often this has more to do with the fact that you just told them they can't go to their friend's party tonight than with how they actually feel about you. When they are all depressed and stating, "I hate my life," it might have more to do with how their toxic parent just made them feel than with how they actually feel about their life. Realizing this might help you to not over-react to their words at the moment.

I found my 14-year old son on the floor of his closet one night. He was curled up in a little ball, laying on his old stuffed animals from childhood, crying. He was repeating over and over, "I hate myself. I hate myself." Why?? Because his dad had trapped him in a lengthy circular conversation that came as a result of our son wanting to watch a different tv show than his father that evening. These horrible conversations, that aren't conversations, leave you feeling drained, worthless and responsible for all the world's problems. I knew he didn't hate himself, and yet it still took a lot of effort to keep myself from flipping out at this scene.

I simply sat with him, on the floor of his closet. I didn't ask what had happened. I didn't ask what all had been said. I just sat with him. He mumbled for a bit about how much he hates his dad. I don't even remember what all he said, but I do remember the pain in his voice and in his heart. He asked if he could go downstairs to our workout room, and he punched on a bag for a while. I kept him company, but again did not push him to talk. I simply made myself present to him and his pain.

Kids need to know that not talking about an issue is okay too. What I have found is when they realize that it truly is okay to not talk, then that is when they are often the most willing to talk. But you have to mean it when you tell them that they don't have to talk with you. That has to be okay, and that is hard to do when you want to help them more than anything else in this world.

Resist the urge to "fix" their feelings. Feelings aren't there to be fixed. Feelings aren't wrong or right. Feelings are feelings. They simply need to be felt. It was perfectly okay for my son to be upset about what had happened. His anger and hurt were justified. If I had tried to persuade him to not be upset, this would only have succeeded in communicating that I didn't think it was okay for him to be upset. It would not have changed the fact that he was upset and would probably have made him more upset.

Instead of trying to fix their feelings, accept their feelings. Validate them. This makes it far easier for your child to feel the way they feel. Once validated, feelings often burn off and settle back down. They just seem to have an overwhelming need to be heard and felt.

Emotional Muscle Building

Kids need emotional muscles in life. Without them, they will certainly suffer in relationships. Think of it this way. If you physically carry your child everywhere in life, they will never learn to walk on their own. Their leg muscles will atrophy and, over a long enough period, walking will no longer be an option for them. This applies emotionally too. If you "fix" everything for them emotionally, then they will never build the emotional muscles that they need.

Quit protecting them from every feeling of disappointment or sadness. Quit protecting them from feeling shame when they deserve it. Quit making them believe that they are above others. Quit rescuing them from the consequences of their actions. Start calling them out on their self-centeredness. Start holding them accountable for their words and actions. Take away their emotional handicaps and create emotional resilience. They are stronger than you think they are. Have confidence in their hearts and in their potential. Carrying them forever only hurts them. Let them work on their muscles in stages while they are still safe in your environment.

No Empty Praise

Kids of toxic parents consistently feel very empty inside. Sometimes we, as parents, add to that emptiness and don't even realize it. When we tell them that they are wonderful and they feel worthless inside, this is empty praise in their ears. We tell them how great they are, how smart they are, how handsome or pretty they are. Even if it's true, it can still be heard as empty. My own kids blew these words off and never believed me. This is because these words do not help them to fill that emptiness inside.

I teach martial arts to kids. I see this empty praise often at my school. A parent will sit in the viewing chairs, with their nose in their phone. They don't pay any attention to what their child is doing in the class. In the meantime, I am having to correct their child repeatedly, calling them out for bad behavior and lack of focus. Much to my surprise though, as we dismiss and the child leaves the floor, the parent will happily exclaim, "Great job today son/daughter. You did great!" I want to say, "Did you see the class? Were you watching how they did?" That child knows they were called out and corrected. They may not be able to verbalize this, but they feel that parent's empty praise for what it is. While they can't put it into words, they know that it doesn't feel right.

While praise may help sometimes, empty praise makes you feel even emptier.

The Feeling of Mattering

When my son was around the age of 10, he had a day that was feeling particularly off to him. He was down and completely unmotivated. He was home all day and completely bored, adding to his lack of motivation. I gave him a small list with a few options of productive things to do. On that list were things like bathe the dogs, vacuum the house, wash the windows, and so on. He decided to bathe the dogs. I was extremely glad he chose that one because it was one chore that I really did not like doing. When he got done, I told him how much I appreciated him doing that and how much it helped me. He actually told me, at that young age, that it had really made him feel better. He felt like he had done something very useful and beneficial. I used this opportunity to teach him about the value of productivity.

On his own, he applied this later in his childhood. As any normal kid does, he had other days when he was off. But he noticed it in himself. So, on his own, he chose to go bathe the dogs. He felt the value of this action and felt like he mattered in our world. He did not need a reward of ice cream, money, or anything else. In fact, sometimes those rewards interfere with a child feeling the more internal rewards. He needed to FEEL productive, helpful, and appreciated. He certainly mattered in my life, but he needed to FEEL that he mattered. Not by my words, but by his actions.

Your kids need to feel that they matter in your world. Don't do this through excessive praise. This so easily gets shallow and meaningless. They need to have chores and responsibilities. They need to feel like a necessary and valuable part of the family. If it is their job to feed the pets, then they need to feed the pets. When they forget, simply remind them and have them do it. Resist the temptation to just do it for them. I know that is quicker and easier, but it does not teach them responsibility and value. Those pets are relying on your kids for their nourishment. Explain that to your child. Most pets will show great appreciation to the one that feeds them. Let your child experience that. It helps them to feel like they matter, which of course, they do.

A Relationship of Trust

You MUST build a relationship of trust with your kids. I am referring to a very specific type of trust here. It is all of the types of trust that are missing in the relationship with a toxic parent.

- Trust that you won't over-react
- Trust that you won't be quickly and easily offended
- Trust that you won't get angry for no apparent reason
- Trust that you won't get angry easily and often
- Trust that your moods do not depend on them
- Trust that you aren't jealous of their time away from you
- Trust that you aren't trying to be the center of their world
- Trust that you won't blame them for things that are not their fault

Go down any list of narcissistic or toxic traits. Your kids need to trust that you aren't going to do these things to them. And you don't need to point it out or "prove" it to them. Remember, that is the kind of behavior that the toxic parent does. They will do something good for you and then be sure to point it out so they get recognized for it. They will adamantly tell you that they aren't angry and then explain why you are the reason for their anger. They will tell you that they don't make life all about them while making it all about them.

Don't defend and explain yourself to your child. Don't point out your good points to them. Just BE the parent that they need – a parent of genuineness, compassion, security, and trust. Kids intuitively know the difference.

As you build this relationship of trust, you now are in a position to **help** with these other crippling feelings. You need to know one thing here. You can't "fix" these internal feelings for them. This is often extremely hard to accept. You want to fix it for them, but you simply can't. You can help them, but they have to do it themselves.

This relationship of trust with you will be one of their single greatest tools. As they trust you more and more, your own actions and attitudes toward them help them to feel worthy and lovable. It helps them to combat the self-doubt. They may start to feel better about themselves and not even realize it. You don't need to point it out to them. Simply let it happen. Let it seem natural and healthy. Let them experience what life and relationships are supposed to be like.

CONCLUSION

When a person shuts their feelings off, this can cause crippling self-doubt. Their self-confidence takes a constant beating as long as their feelings stay closed up. Helping your child open their vault of feelings is one of the best things you can do for them. Scary! But best!

I was in my 40's when I declared, "It is time for my internal world to meet my external world." Up to this point, I had been a different person on the inside of me than the one I showed to the world. The internal conflict this caused was intense, and yet easily overlooked. Slowly I started dropping the inhibitions and opening myself to the world around me. I quickly realized that it was extremely freeing. I sincerely want my boys to find this freedom too.

Give them the space to explore their feelings. It might be a tough ride, so hang on. But it will be so worth it in the long run!

PERSONAL NOTES

THE CHILD'S STUNTED EMOTIONAL DEVELOPMENT

INTRODUCTION

There is NO doubt that children of toxic parents suffer emotionally. Their emotional development often is severely stunted. Because of this the child might not develop the skills necessary for building healthy emotional connections life. Unfortunately this can carry well into their adulthood years and greatly affect their future relationships.

Narcissism can too easily carry from one generation to the next. When I married my husband, I had no idea what narcissism even was. I did not see it in him or his father. After having 2 kids with him and being married for many years, I knew that something was terribly wrong. There seemed to be a massive block in the way of our relationship. Since then I have now learned what that block is - covert narcissism. And there is a cycle of it in his family.

Seeing this trend of narcissism and beginning to see signs of it in my own boys nearly panicked me. I began researching as much as I possibly could, desperately seeking ways to break this cycle. In this searching, I found some extremely useful information, and it needs to be available to ALL parents.

CHILDHOOD EMOTIONAL INJURIES

Traumatic injury, especially in childhood, often brings one's emotional growth to a screaming halt. It can leave the individual trapped in the emotional stage of that age group. In this situation, they still grow physically and mentally, but not emotionally. For example, if a severe emotional trauma happens to an individual in their early teenage years and they do not receive help processing it, then that person possibly never develops past the emotional capacity of a young teenager. This is when you find yourself dealing with a full-grown adult yet feeling like you are dealing with a teenager in their reactions to you.

Childhood injuries vary in type and severity. It can be the death of a loved one, moving cities leaving close friends behind, or even emotional or physical abuse by a parent. When these traumas are more than the child can handle, one of the common reactions is for that child to shut their hearts off in self-protection. They hide behind an internal protective wall. This can certainly cause many relationship problems in their future. If they remain emotionally stuck, this leads to the even greater potential of developing narcissism or other personality disorders in adulthood.

SURROUND YOURSELF WITH SUPPORT

Helping children heal from toxic abuse is NO SMALL TASK! You have possibly heard the saying, "It takes a community to raise a child." This statement is very true, especially in toxic family situations. The community has two different aspects, though, one for you and one for your child.

When dealing with a toxic partner, you are going to need a support group for yourself. The path you are on is extremely frustrating, and you need at least a few friends or family to whom you can vent. These need to be people who "get it." Explaining narcissism or other toxic behavior to someone is NOT easy. You either sound like a lunatic or a petty crybaby. Regardless, you must open up to a few people you trust. A therapist experienced with this toxic environment is also incredibly helpful.

This need for support is no different for your child. They are also going to experience others not really getting it when they try to talk about what is going on. This is extremely frustrating and invalidating. If at all possible, help your child to have some genuine adult connections in their lives. These connections can be teachers, sports' coaches, church leaders, grandparents, other family members, or even the parents of their friends. Choose 1 or 2 that you truly trust and that your child seems to really connect with. Give that adult some understanding of what is going on in your home. You are not asking anything of them, other than that they love and support your child. Kids of toxic parents need allies in life, even though they may not realize it yet. Let your kids know who those adults are, so they know they are free to talk with them. Also don't rule out a good counselor or therapist, even at a young age.

Secrets hurt individuals and families. The natural tendency is to hide the abuse. We pretend that nothing is wrong. Showing a positive face to the world may be easier, but it is suicidal. In the long run, these secrets do incredible damage.

Let your kids know that it is okay to talk about what is going on. Encourage them to open up with their friends. Let them know who you are open with. Even let them hear you talking with that trusted friend about some of this.

THE HEALING PROCESS

As I have mentioned several times in my books, you must begin your own process of healing. If you are still a basket of raw, injured emotions, then there is no way that you are going to actually be able to help your children. For more on this, read book 2 in this series, Making a Plan.

The Healing Process
- Identify an injury from your past
- Identify the feelings inside you from this injury
- Name these feelings, be specific - sadness, anger, confusion, shame, fear
- Spend some time with these feelings
- Accept these feelings for what they are

- Give yourself permission to feel this way right now
- Learn from the feelings
- See yourself as a stronger person because of these feelings and what they have taught you
- Let the feelings float away with awareness and gratitude

For an added visual, you can do something more hands on. Get a piece of paper. Write down these injuries and the feelings it caused in you. Then safely burn that piece of paper. Watch it go up in flames. Or you can get a bottle. Speak the injuries and feelings into that bottle. Put a lid or cork on it. Then dispose of that bottle. Yes, these feelings will return some. But when they do, you will have a strong visual memory of the release of these injuries and feelings. Use that memory as a tool to continue getting further and further from them. It is a part of your healing.

You need to learn this process and practice it yourself. You need to feel the benefits first-hand. Copy these steps down. Pull it out every day. If you are or were in a toxic relationship, then you will have no problem remembering past injuries. There are plenty to choose from. Pick one and get started. As you become more experienced with this process, you will find yourself doing it more automatically, even immediately as an injury occurs. GREAT! That is a really good place to be.

Teach the Process to Your Child

As you become more acquainted with the process, begin introducing it to your child. These steps can even be done with very young children. You might encourage them to draw their feelings in pictures. Then they can destroy the pictures of the negative feelings, giving themselves permission to release them. Older kids might not be inclined to draw. You can turn to journaling or even simply talking about it.

We all know that the older kids get, the more closed off they become to their parents. So start this at a young age with your kids. If you are just now reading this and they are already teenagers, it isn't too late. It will take a bit more pushing though. They may be resistant and get frustrated, but that's okay. Let them express that frustration. It is still better for them to put voice even to that feeling than to bottle everything up inside.

When your teenager closes up, don't panic. They all do this. Give them some space too. But keep loving them. Keep reaching out to them. And above all, keep providing an emotionally safe environment for them. They will come back.

ABILITY TO HANDLE FEELINGS

We all experience strong feelings. Unfortunately for many of us, these feelings are too overwhelming for us, so we run from them. We bottle them up and stuff them away. We hide them from the world and pretend that everything is okay. Not only that, but we teach our kids to do this as well. Our inability to handle our own feelings continues to pass from generation to generation.

It is time to break this vicious cycle! Start connecting with your own feelings. Acknowledge them, pay attention to them, and feel them. No more hiding! As you get better at this, you open the door for your kids to as well. Remember this path is for you and for your kids.

Simply start noticing your feelings. How do you feel today? Ask yourself this continuously throughout your day. Feelings change often, so stay conscious of this question. Don't judge your feelings. They are what they are. Just pay attention to them. Give them a name: happy, sad, nervous, scared, angry, joyous, and so on.

Allow the feelings to exist. It is okay to be scared or angry. It is also okay to be happy or joyous. Name them out loud. Simply say, "I feel sad right now." You don't have to try to figure out why. Sometimes our feelings don't make sense. Explanations often just bog us down and get in the way. They make us think too much. You don't have to blame your feelings on anything.

Self-Regulation

We all experience strong emotions. Learning to self-regulate those emotions is crucial for healthy relationships. For example, anger can cause us to do things that we normally wouldn't do. Remember the first step is noticing your feelings. Recognize that you are angry. If you aren't even aware of it, you will never be able to self-regulate it.

Then, you need to work on internal filters that check your reactions. Practice looking at your own reactions as though you were a stranger looking in. If you decide your reaction was not reasonable, then take the necessary steps to make it right. If you have hurt someone with your words, go to them and simply apologize. Don't pass the blame. Don't even blame your anger. Just own it and apologize, forgiving yourself too.

As you get better at noticing your own feelings, your ability to self-regulate them will be stronger too. When you know that you are experiencing anger, your awareness of that will help you to keep your reactions in check.

Tools for Stabilizing Emotions

Build a toolbox and teach your kids to do the same. Here are some things you will want in this toolbox.

A music playlist on your phone

Make separate playlists on your phone or other device for various negative feelings you face, such as anger, sadness, anxiety, and so on. Put in songs that help you get through these tough feelings. They should be songs that allow you to feel those feelings, not just songs that push you to be happy. It is important that you allow yourself to feel the negative feeling before moving on. You might find a combination of song types to work best for you. Experiment with your playlists. Only use them when you are in need of them. Keep them special for those times, especially if you are dealing with extremely strong emotions.

A comfort item, such as a blanket or stuffed animal

You might find a comfort item to be useful. When you are feeling sad, this comfort item can be extremely useful. It allows you to just feel sad for a while. Remember, there is nothing wrong with that. As silly as it may seem to some, this is a great way to give yourself permission to feel sad.

A physical activity

Some feelings work best with physical activity, such as running, walking, working out, punching a workout bag, aerobics, dancing, and even cleaning. All of these can have a tremendous therapeutic effect for our feelings.

A friend to turn to

If you are struggling with facing tough emotions, a friend that you feel completely safe talking with is a great tool. We all need friends who are able to accept us, even at our worst. We need friends who love us, especially when we feel unlovable. Know who these friends are, and please, don't hesitate to turn to them. Tell them how you are feeling. They don't need to "fix" anything. They simply need to listen. The goal here is allowing your feelings to exist.

Be sure to return the favor to them as well. Allow them to feel their feelings around you. Be that safe person who won't judge them, admonish them or try to fix them. Friendships like this are crucial to everyone's emotional growth and development.

THE DIFFERENCE OF ONE HEALTHY CONNECTION

Toxic people do NOT build healthy emotional connections with anyone. Not with you, their kids, their own parents, friends, or co-workers. No one! Kids who suffer under them carry the risk of continuing this cycle.

The good news is that it only takes one significant person in their life to counter this damage. You, the counter-parent, can be that person. You must allow them to experience a healthy emotional connection with you.

Consider everything we have talked about in these books. Read everything you can get your hands on regarding healthy parenting, as well as on toxic and even narcissistic parenting. Work on your own emotional stability and health. Trust your heart as you walk through this with your child.

No matter what roadblocks and struggles come, you will get through it. You will have good days and bad days, just like everyone else. Remember your goal is a healthy emotional connection. Your goal is not a child who is never angry or upset. Your goal is not a child who is perfect and happy all the time. These goals cause more problems, not less.

You Are NOT Special

This may sound harsh, but you are not special and neither are your kids. We all are injured by others in life. Your injuries don't make you any more special than anyone else. At the same time, their injuries don't make them any more special than anyone else either. Every feeling you have ever felt has been experienced by billions of people before. THIS IS NOTHING NEW UNDER THE SUN!

People have been hurting each other for thousands of generations. If you think that no one else understands your pain, YOU ARE WRONG! Thousands of people understand your pain. Maybe you haven't met any of them, but I assure you that they are out there. Perhaps people you even know right now, but no one is talking about their pain. We humans are very good at secretly carrying around large amounts of pain.

Don't treat yourself or your kids as "special." Their wounds do not give them the right to treat others badly, and the earlier they realize this, the better off they will be. Pain is NO excuse to start hurting others, but too many people use it that way. So despite all the advice given when I was a kid, DO NOT teach your kids that they are special.

They may be special in your eyes, and that's fine. Even Grandma's and Grandpa's can think they are special. But to the world, they are no different than anyone else, and ultimately they must know this.

You are NOT a superhero!

Please remember too that you are no different than any other parent struggling through parenthood. I got wrapped up in trying to make sure I did everything right for my kids. I so badly wanted to, as I'm sure you do. I don't question your desire to be a great parent. That is a wonderful desire. But it is easy to get so caught up in trying to do everything right that we end up doing everything wrong.

Give yourself permission to be human. You can't fix everything. You can't help them with everything. This isn't all bad. They NEED to learn some things for themselves as well. They NEED to learn to rely on themselves. That's okay.

If someone would have just told me what to do in order to ensure my boys have a bright, healthy and happy future, I would have walked through fire for them. Trouble is that there is no blueprint, no sure way, and no guidebook with all the answers. You do the best you can and then you let them go. Trust your heart and learn to trust theirs too!

Your goal is simply a healthy emotional connection with your child, so they can learn to create healthy emotional connections in their life.

Purposefully Forgive Yourself

As we have already talked about, one of the absolute best ways to help your kids is to work on you. Your own healing and strength give your kids a secure place to turn to when they are ready. They need you! They need a healthy you!

In order to find that healing in you, you must forgive yourself. This is hard, especially when you feel so responsible for the pain you see in your kids. I know. I have lived this myself, for years. You have to dig deep in your heart and forgive yourself.

Your kids also carry a lot of internal blame. They blame themselves for all the pain and problems. It doesn't matter how much you try to tell them this isn't their fault. There seems to be a script that is written for children of abuse. They need you to lead the way through the forgiveness.

Make a list of all the things you need to forgive yourself for. Mine looks like this:

- Forgive myself for bringing these boys into this abusive situation
- Forgive myself for not seeing it sooner
- Forgive myself for letting him treat me and the boys this way
- Forgive myself for not being able to stop it
- Forgive myself for not being able to help my boys more
- Forgive myself for sweeping everything under the rug
- Forgive myself for not having all the answers
- Forgive myself for not being the superhero

As soon as you accept this, you are forgiven. It is that simple. It is okay that you didn't have all the answers. It is okay that you didn't know what to do. No one decided that you had to be "God" and fix everything. So forgive yourself and let it all go, now.

TOOLS FOR BUILDING HEALTHY CONNECTIONS

Your kids need the tools necessary for building healthy connections in life. In a healthy and stable home environment, they learn these by watching the interactions between mom and dad. Unfortunately, in a toxic home, this learning does not take place.

I will never forget a conversation I had with my 18-year old son. He told me that as a youngster, he concluded that marriage was a difficult chore in life. He just accepted that it was like that for everyone. He expected that in his future, this was one of the hardships he would have to endure. He said that he didn't realize that relationships could be fun and enjoyable.

This absolutely broke my heart. I sincerely apologized to him and told him that healthy relationships are a wonderful thing. Yes, they are still work, but they are rewarding because you work and grow together.

When your kids are not learning about healthy connections at home, you need to be much more attuned to helping them build the necessary skills. What are these skills?

Positive Reciprocity

Reciprocity is the give and take in a relationship. It can be positive or negative. Let's take a look at the negative way reciprocity can play out.

Negative reciprocity can also be called revenge. Even with people we love, we all do things that hurt each other. That is a part of our humanness. When this has happened and the partner responds with an equally negative behavior, this is negative reciprocity. It is a reaction with the intent of "getting even." The attitude might be, "I'll show you." This has an incredibly damaging effect on the relationship and will only succeed in destroying it.

Positive reciprocity, on the other hand, is a spirit of cooperation. It is when you give each other the space to make mistakes. You both offer and receive each other's forgiveness mutually. Both partners must be able to take personal responsibility for their own actions and attitudes. Passing blame kills positive reciprocity. When you develop these skills, they take your relationship to amazing levels of depth and trust.

Relationships have a natural flow to them. When one partner is carrying all the weight of the relationship, this is not sustainable. One partner cannot do all the work, whether this is the physical work around the house, the parental duties of raising the kids, or even the emotional work of maintaining a strong connection. Both partners must be engaged in the work of the family and both partners must be allowed time and space to truly rest.

Ability to forgive and receive forgiveness

One huge aspect of positive reciprocity is the ability to forgive each other and to receive each other's forgiveness. Both parts of this must happen. Saying you are sorry takes you to a place of vulnerability. Accepting that apology provides safety for that vulnerability. Both parts of this allow trust to be developed and the relationship to strengthen.

Recognize the value of using fewer words! When you say, "I'm sorry," keep is simple, genuine, and short.

Following the apology with an explanation or description only creates problems. Do NOT recreate the situation or try to relive it in any way! Even with the best of intentions, this will take both people back to the hurt feelings and is extremely counter-productive.

At the same time, when you are receiving an apology, use few words here too. A simple, "Thank you" has so much value to it. Again, don't give any explanations or try to relive the situation that created the problem in the first place.

With the apology and its reception, you are both creating a new environment, one of safety, trust, and connection. Enjoy this space and allow your child to value it for what it is. This space of trust is the ultimate goal.

Ability to take responsibility and not pass blame

This is vital to a healthy relationship. It goes hand in hand with forgiveness and is another aspect of positive reciprocity. With your own actions and words, show your child how to take personal responsibility. Be quick to ask for their forgiveness when you have hurt them. As a parent, I assure you that you have stepped on their feelings from time to time. Own it. Apologize for it. Don't make excuses or pass the blame. This is another reason to use few words when offering an apology. It is simply too easy for extra words to sound like and even become passing the blame.

Teach your kids to own their actions and words. Do not allow them to make excuses or find ways to justify things. When they have hurt someone, they should apologize. This has nothing to do with whether they meant to hurt them or not. Even when we accidentally hurt someone, we absolutely should apologize.

Let your kids know that there is no shame in an apology. Too often, when an adult is telling a child they need to apologize, the adult is speaking with anger and frustration. The firmness in their voice communicates shame to the child. It is not necessary to be angry in order to teach your child to apologize. Teach them that there is honor in apologizing.

Ability to self-reflect honestly and openly

In order to build healthy relationships, both partners must practice genuine self-reflection. If you think that you are right all the time and your partner is wrong, then you are not being realistic or cooperative. On the same note, though, if you think that you are wrong all the time and your partner is right all the time, this also is not realistic or supporting cooperation.

To build healthy connections, you must work on the skill of looking at your interactions objectively. This is not always easy, especially when emotions are high. If you are always demanding your way, then you need to take a serious look at yourself. And if you are always sweeping everything under the rug, then you also need to take a serious look at yourself. Both extremes are a disaster to a relationship.

Teach your kids that it is okay to voice their opinions, even if they differ from others. They have not learned this from their toxic parent. In fact, they have learned to keep their mouth shut and their thoughts to themselves. If they carry this into their future relationships, they will suffer. Help them to see that they need to work on this. Give them safety with you, so they can practice voicing their own thoughts.

Teach your kids that it is okay to find faults and weaknesses within themselves. This does not make them a failure or worthless in any way. This can be tough for them. A toxic parent often leaves their child feeling incredibly worthless. So when the child feels any of that feeling inside, it often causes them to shut down and even hate themselves.

Talk about this at a time when they are feeling emotionally safe and strong. Let them see faults and weaknesses in you. Talk about these with them. Share with your kids how you are learning and growing in life. Again, at a time when they are feeling emotionally secure with you, ask them what weaknesses they see in themselves. Let them voice these. Explore ways they might improve. Do this in baby steps. If they start to shut down, be ready to shift gears. Remember you want this to be a positive experience for them, so they will be willing to return.

Take everything in small steps. It will seem painfully slow at times. You will seem to take 3 steps forward and 3 steps back on a regular basis. And if they are teenagers, hang on. It is a heck of a ride!

I have come to the realization that my life will never be boring with my two boys in it! I'm okay with that most of the time. But sometimes I have to remind myself to breathe. It helps so much knowing that so many people have traveled this journey in front of me and many more come behind me. You and I are not alone!

CONCLUSION

You are stronger than you think you are! I am not going to tell you that this will be an easy journey. It will almost certainly not be. But you can do it, and you will be even stronger because of it.

Teach your child all that you can. Give them all the tools you are capable of for a successful life. You are taking positive steps to help your child right now. But don't ever forget that you are only human and not responsible to fix everything or to have all the answers. You will make some mistakes along the way. That's okay, and you need to accept this.

I know we are talking about your child. I understand how strong that connection is. I get it! I would give my life for either of my boys, without hesitation. But please remember, you birthed a human being. They are a person, just like anyone else in this world. They have their own journey to travel in life, and so do you.

They will struggle, and so will you. They will succeed sometimes, and they will fail other times. They will have ups and downs, just like everyone else in this world. They are not exempt.

Of all the phases of parenthood that I have lived and survived, the hardest one by far is letting go. This is where trust becomes so vitally important. You have to trust that you did everything you could at the time to help them. Trust that they have it from here. Trust that life will continue to put people in their lives to help them along the way. Trust that they will continue to learn and grow.

Your kids will learn so much in this life, and they have you to thank for putting them on a healthy path. Someday they will understand the value of all you have done for them. That may take a while, so be patient. And in the meantime, just keep moving forward, one step at a time.

PERSONAL NOTES

_____

_____

_____

_____

_____

_____

_____

_____

_____

_____

_____

_____

_____

_____

_____

_____

_____

_____

_____

_____

_____

Renee Swanson

Email: renee@universallyus.com

Website: www.universallyus.com
www.covertnarcissism.com

Facebook:
https://www.facebook.com/renee.covertnarcissism

Closed Facebook Group:
https://www.facebook.com/groups/covertnarcissism/

Made in the USA
Monee, IL
27 February 2020